The BIBLE
Project Book

MERYL DONEY

HODDER AND STOUGHTON

LONDON   SYDNEY   AUCKLAND   TORONTO

What a book!

The Bible is one of the most remarkable books in the world. It is certainly the best known and the world's oldest best-seller.

- The Bible appears in *The Guiness Book of Records* three times.

- It was the first-ever book to be printed by machine (see page 24). Only 21 of these first printed Bibles have survived. In 1978 one was sold for a record £1 265 000.

- In the 160 years between 1815 and 1975, a staggering two-and-a-half billion copies of the Bible were sold throughout the world!

The story of the Bible covers more than four thousand years. All kinds of people, from different times, races and backgrounds have been involved. People have argued about the Bible's message and even fought wars over it. Others have risked their lives to translate it into everyday language.

The Bible Project Book

In this book, we'll be looking at the Bible, what it's about, who wrote it, and why, and at its long and exciting history.

As well as all this information, there are projects to tackle, things to make and do, places to visit and lots of ideas to help you get involved.

You will need a Bible to help you with some of the projects in this book. If you don't already have one, look at page 29 for help in choosing your own.

If you look at the back cover of this book, you'll find a book mark for you to cut out. One side of it has a list of well-known or useful parts of the Bible. On the back, there is space for you to fill in your name and the page numbers from your own Bible. Use the marker to help you find your way around.

It's all in the Bible

It's surprising how many of the things we say and do, come from the Bible.

'Good grief! There's no peace for the wicked.'

'You Judas!'

'In my job, I need the wisdom of Solomon and the patience of Job!'

'Phew, I just made it – by the skin of my teeth!'

'He's living on the fat of the land.'

Many of these sayings come from the old Authorised (or King James) version of the Bible. Today we have many more versions to choose from. In this book we are using the *New International Bible*.

Why have people always taken at least one working day off, out of seven? (Many of us have both Saturday and Sunday off nowadays, but this is fairly recent.)

This comes from the story of the creation of the world, at the beginning of the Bible. In Genesis, Chapter 2 it says, '. . . after all his work, God rested on the seventh day.'

Among the Jewish people, no one – not even slaves – had to work on the seventh day, the Sabbath.

We took the idea from them. In fact, several countries have tried to make people work for longer without a break, but it has never been successful.

Why is the dove used as a sign of peace?

This comes from the story of Noah and the ark. When the great flood had gone, Noah sent out a dove. It came back with an olive leaf in its beak to show that trees were beginning to grow again. God had made peace with the world. You can find this story in Genesis, Chapter 6.

Something to do

Many children are named after characters in the Bible. Are there any in your family or in your class in school?

Jessica means 'the rich one'

Philip means 'lover of horses'

Sarah means 'princess'

Andrew means 'strong and manly'

Look in a book of names, or a Bible Encyclopaedia to see who your friends are named after and what the name means.

Totally trivial teasers

(from the Authorised Version of the Bible)

- Someone has counted every letter in the Bible. There are 3 566 480.

- The shortest verse is John 11, verse 35. It says 'Jesus wept.'

- The very middle of the Bible comes in Psalm 118, verse 8.

- The word 'and' comes 35 543 times in the Old Testament and 10 684 in the New Testament.

- Ezra 7 verse 21 contains all the letters of the alphabet except J.

Finding your way about the Bible

Take a good look at your own Bible. What kind of book is it?

To begin with, the cover may not be very interesting. A few versions have picture covers, but most have only a simple title on the front. Older Bibles used to be bound in red or black leather. They had gold letters and sometimes a cross.

Open your Bible and look at the first few pages. Some have useful information, maps or pictures. Some have a place for you to write your name and details about yourself.

A typical Bible page

To help people find parts of the Bible easily, it has been divided up into short chunks called chapters. These are each numbered at the beginning.

Each chapter is then divided into verses. These have smaller numbers.

There is usually a 'Preface' which tells you about how and why your particular version was written.

Now look at the 'Contents' page. It will give you a list of all the books in the Bible with their page numbers. Some versions include a contents list in alphabetical order. This is a great help if you don't know the Bible very well.

From the list of contents, you will see that the Bible is divided up into two parts: the Old Testament (with 39 'books') and the New Testament (with 27 'books').

Difficult words usually have a small letter by them, and are explained at the bottom of the page.

Chapter and verse

You can find any sentence in the Bible, simply by looking up its reference, which is written like this:

> 1 Corinthians 13:4–7

The title of the book is 1 Corinthians. (There are two books called Corinthians, 1 Corinthians and 2 Corinthians. We want the first one.)

The chapter number is 13.

The verses to read are 4 to 7.

Where it all happened

All the events covered by the Bible took place in a part of the world called today 'the Near East'.

Most of the Old Testament is the story of the family of Abraham. They were known as the Hebrews (meaning 'those from beyond').

Later they were called Israelites and later still, the Jews.

They settled in the land at the Eastern end of the Mediterranean Sea, called Canaan.

Once they took over, the land became known as Israel. Later, the Greeks and Romans called the country Palestine. The Israelites also called it the 'promised land' because they believed God had given it to them.

This narrow strip of land has always been important because it is a link between Africa and the great continents to the North and East. Since earliest times, traders have travelled through the country, making it a centre of the ancient world.

A code to crack

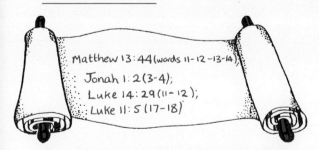

Matthew 13:44 (words 11-12-13-14),
Jonah 1:2 (3-4);
Luke 14:29 (11-12);
Luke 11:5 (17-18)

Pirate Jake needs to get a secret message to Lady Claire. He knows she has a Good News Bible. He gives her this coded message. Can you find out what it says?
(answer on page 32)

The Bible World Today

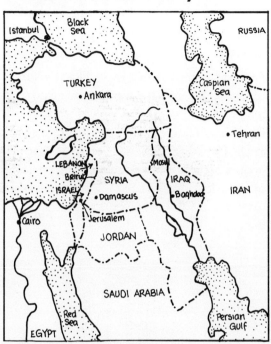

Something to make

Make these Mystery Bible Cakes and treat your family.

(Check what you think is the real receipe with the answer on page 32 before you start to make the cakes!)

Take 4oz Proverbs 30:33, (first half)
1 desertspoonful of Revelation 10:10, and 3oz sugar.
Mix them together.
Add 2 Jeremiah 17:11,
4oz self-raising 1 Kings 4:22,
and ½ teaspoon baking powder.
Mix it all together and drop the mixture into bun tins or paper cases.
Bake in the oven 190°C (375°F) Gas Mark 5 for about 15 mins.
When cool, spread with a little Revelation 10:10 and decorate with 1 Samuel 29:2

A library of books

At first sight, the Bible looks like the sort of storybook you are sometimes given for birthdays. But once you look at it more closely, you find out that it is not one book at all. The Bible is a collection of 66 books, brought together over a very long period of time. It contains stories, history, poetry, plays, hymns and even some personal letters.

The Old Testament

The first five books are called the Law or the Torah in Hebrew. They are also called the Pentateuch, which means 'five scrolls'. It is really one book, divided into five parts. It covers the history of the people of Israel from the very beginning to the time of Moses.

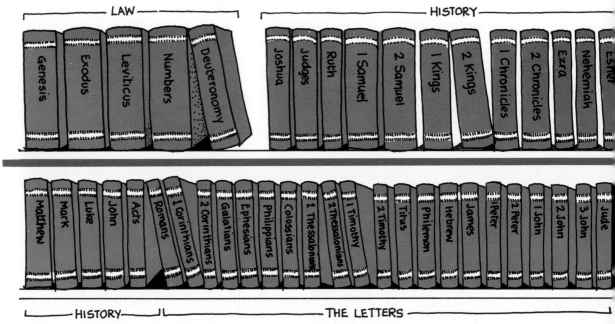

LAW — Genesis, Exodus, Leviticus, Numbers, Deuteronomy

HISTORY — Joshua, Judges, Ruth, 1 Samuel, 2 Samuel, 1 Kings, 2 Kings, 1 Chronicles, 2 Chronicles, Ezra, Nehemiah, Esther

Matthew, Mark, Luke, John, Acts, Romans, 1 Corinthians, 2 Corinthians, Galatians, Ephesians, Philippians, Colossians, 1 Thessalonians, 2 Thessalonians, 1 Timothy, 2 Timothy, Titus, Philemon, Hebrew, James, Peter, 2 Peter, 1 John, 2 John, 3 John, Jude

HISTORY — THE LETTERS

NEW TESTAMENT

The New Testament

The first five New Testament books are also history. The four gospels tell the story of Jesus. The Acts of the Apostles is the story of the first Christians.

The next twenty-one books are really letters sent out to the small groups of Christians called churches. They are named after the people (or the town) to whom they were sent.

The last book is a strange dream about the future. It is meant to remind people that God is in control of everything that happens in the universe. It was written to encourage the first Christians, who were having a hard time.

The next twelve are books of history. They take the story on from Moses and Joshua to the end of Old Testament times.

In the middle of The Bible are five books of poetry, plays, hymns and wise sayings.

The last seventeen books of the Old Testament are called the Prophets. A prophet was someone sent by God to give a message to the people. These books tell us about them and the message they preached.

This is what the Bible would look like, set out as a library of books.

OLD TESTAMENT

WISDOM — Job Psalms Proverbs Ecclesiastes Song of Songs

THE PROPHETS — Isaiah Jeremiah Lamentations Ezekiel Daniel Hosea Joel Amos Obadiah Jonah Micah Nahum Habakkuk Zephaniah Haggai Zechariah Malachi

Something to make

Make a special file, shaped like a book, to hold all your Bible project work. Carefully open your next large cereal packet, without tearing it. When the box is empty, re-close the packet with sticky tape so it looks like a closed book. Next, cut around three sides of the box front so it flaps open like a front cover. Don't cut right up to the closed left hand edge. Leave about 25mm uncut.

My Bible Project File

John Smith

CORNFLAKES

CUT

fold

CUT

CUT

Cover the front and back of the file with the nicest wrapping paper you can find. Stick a long strip of white paper around three of the packet sides and draw lines on them to look like pages. Stick a piece of plain coloured paper round the left side of the box, overlapping 25mm on either side. Write your name and a title on the spine and front cover of your 'book' file.

Background to the Bible

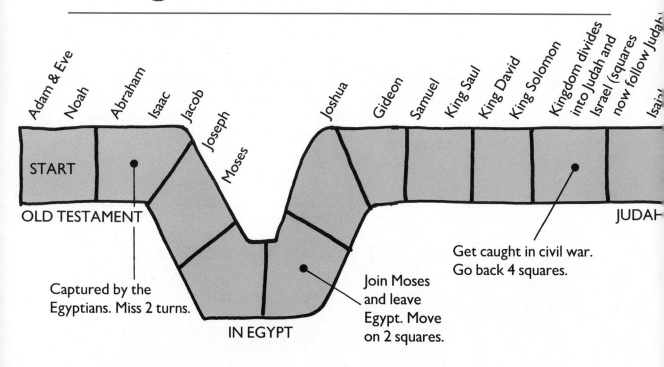

Adam & Eve · Noah · Abraham · Isaac · Jacob · Joseph · Moses · Joshua · Gideon · Samuel · King Saul · King David · King Solomon · Kingdom divides into Judah and Israel (squares now follow Judah) · Isaiah

START

OLD TESTAMENT

IN EGYPT

JUDAH

Captured by the Egyptians. Miss 2 turns.

Join Moses and leave Egypt. Move on 2 squares.

Get caught in civil war. Go back 4 squares.

A game to play

Here's a 'bird's-eye view' of the story of God's people in the Bible. It shows where the various well-known characters fit in. Use it to play a game with two or three friends. You will need a die and some small counters (different coloured buttons will do).

Each person has a counter. Throw the die in turn and move your counter according to your score. Obey the instructions as you go. The first player to reach the end square by throwing the exact right number is the winner.

Walk like an Egyptian!

Dress up like an Egyptian king or 'pharaoh'. Wrap a striped towel over your hair and fasten it behind your head, letting the sides hang down. Draw and colour the head of a cobra snake on a piece of paper. Cut it out and tuck it under the front of the towel. Use eyeliner to make up your eyes.

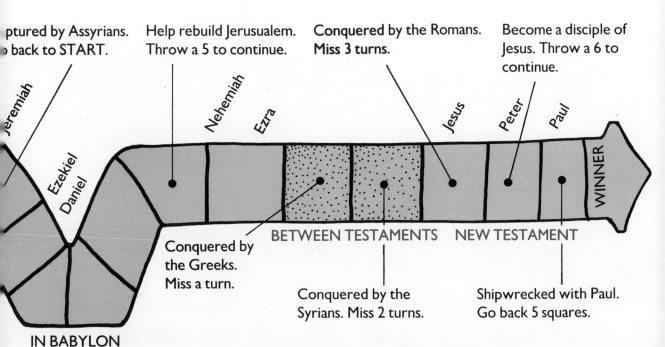

ptured by Assyrians. back to START.

Help rebuild Jerusualem. Throw a 5 to continue.

Conquered by the Romans. **Miss 3 turns.**

Become a disciple of Jesus. Throw a 6 to continue.

Jeremiah

Ezekiel
Daniel

Nehemiah

Ezra

Jesus

Peter

Paul

WINNER

IN BABYLON

Conquered by the Greeks. Miss a turn.

BETWEEN TESTAMENTS

NEW TESTAMENT

Conquered by the Syrians. Miss 2 turns.

Shipwrecked with Paul. Go back 5 squares.

Be a Greek soldier

Make a Greek soldier's helmet from an empty cereal packet. Open the box at both ends and cut it to shape. Close the top over your head with sticky tape and paint in dark gold to look like bronze. You could also make a sword or spear and a round shield using the card from empty boxes.

Project: ancient people

During the Old Testament, Israel was sandwiched between the great powers Assyria and Babylon in the North and Egypt to the South. By New Testament times, Israel had been conquered by the Greeks, the Syrians and the Romans. Of these, the Greeks made the most lasting impression. By Jesus' day, many Jews had taken Greek names, wore greek-style clothes and spoke the language. Most of the New Testament was written in Greek.

Find out all you can about these people and how they lived.

From rocks to books!

Long before paper was invented, people wrote on all kinds of things. They painted on the walls of caves or scratched the surface of a smooth piece of rock.

People soon found that clay, dug from the earth, could be made into shapes and dried in the sun. They made pots and bowls for their houses from this clay. They also wrote on pieces of pottery.

Writing on pottery, about 600 BC

Clay tablets

People found it difficult to draw curved lines on wet clay. They found a simple way of making letters with a stick shaped like a triangle at the end. This type of writing is called 'cuneiform'.

We still write on pottery today. Plates and cups are made to mark special occasions. Beautiful handwriting may be used. This art of handwriting is called 'calligraphy'.

Something to make

Make a permanent record of your family. Have an adult help you to sharpen the end of an old pencil into a triangle shape. Press the pencil end onto rolled-out clay, marking lots of triangles to form letters. Write the names of people in your family this way, and the date. Leave the clay slab in a warm, dry place to harden.

Something to do

Ask if you can have a plain white saucer or plate to decorate. Use a thin brush dipped in model-making paint. Write your name and the date round the edge. (If you want to use the plate for food you will need to buy special paint which can be hardened in the oven.)

Paper

The English word 'paper' comes from a reed called papyrus. People discovered that they could cut the stems of papyrus into thin strips. These strips could be beaten together to make flat sheets for writing.

Something to make

You can make new paper out of old newspaper very simply. Tear some sheets of newspaper into tiny pieces and soak them in a bucket of water. Pound the mixture to a pulp with a wooden spoon. Pour the pulp into a cooking sieve and press so the water drips out. Gently spread the pulp flat with the back of a spoon. Leave it to dry in a warm place. When the pulp is completely dry your new paper will peel off the sieve. Roll it out flat with a rolling pin and trim it square.

The Scroll

People soon discovered that they could keep long manuscripts by making a strip of papyrus and rolling it round two pieces of smooth wood. This kind of 'book' was called a scroll. It was light to carry and easy to read. The Old Testament books were all made this way.

The Book

The first Christians may have been the people who invented the book as we know it. The stories about what Jesus said and did were very important to them. They took these writings wherever they went so they needed a safe way to carry them. They hit upon the idea of folding the paper into a stack and sewing it together down one side. A cover was added later, to protect the paper.

The Codex Sinaiticus is a book made in

this way. It is the earliest complete manuscript of the New Testament. It is kept in the Manuscript Saloon, Room 30, of the British Museum in London.

Writing it down

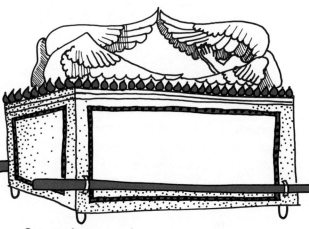

Long before writing was invented, people would gather round the fire after a meal and tell stories. It was their only way of passing on family history.

When writing began, the stories were copied down faithfully time after time.

The story of the people of Israel was kept in this way too. The Old Testament is one of the oldest documents of recorded history.

A clue to how the Old Testament was collected together comes in a very old book of Jewish history called Maccabes. It says that Nehemiah, one of the last leaders of the Jewish people mentioned in the Old Testament . . . 'founded a library, gathered together the books about the kings and prophets, and the books of David and letters of kings about sacred gifts.'

Project: The Lost Ark

Have you heard of the Ten Commandments? They were the laws God gave to Moses for his people to follow. The Bible says they were carved on both sides of two stone blocks. These were kept in the special Covenant (agreement) Box or Ark of the Covenant in the tent where God was worshipped. This Covenant Box was featured in the film *Raiders of the Lost Ark*. No one knows exactly what it looked like, but it was a box with carrying poles, made of acacia wood, and covered with gold. The lid was a gold plate carved with two winged cherubs on either end.

Something to do

Find out all you can about the real thing. A Bible Encyclopedia and Dictionary will help. Look up these Bible verses: Exodus 25:1–22; 40:16–21. Write all your discoveries in a small notebook.

Make a model of the Ark. Take an oblong box, big enough to hold the book. Close the ends with sticky tape and cut round three sides of the top, so that it opens.

On another piece of card, draw round the end of the box and add rings and legs. Cut out two of these shapes and stick them to either end of the box.

Make the lid from yellow plasticine. Roll out a flat rectangle to fit the top of the box. Make two cherubs, like lions with big wings. These go on the lid, facing each other.

Paint the whole box gold or yellow and slot two sticks through the loops to make carrying poles.

Scribes

A scribe in the 15th century AD

As there was no printing in Bible times, scribes were the people who had the important job of copying books. They had very strict rules about how to do this. A scribe must not make a single mistake. When he had finished copying something, he had to count the exact number of lines and check them with the original. Then a second scribe would check his work.

Letters by hand

The first parts of the New Testament to be written down were the letters. They were written by Paul and other leaders to help the scattered groups of Jesus' followers.

These letters were so important to the early Christians that they kept them very safely.

A game to play

Play this game to see how good you are at copying.

Get several people in a line with you. Whisper a short message to the person next to you. Then ask them to pass it on. When it reaches the last person in the line, ask them to repeat the message they heard out loud. It is often quite different from the first message!

Something to do

Write a special letter to someone. Practise your signature until you can do it well. Before putting your letter in an envelope, make it look very old. Fold it twice. Then fold in the sides. Melt a blob of sealing wax (bought from a stationer's) over a candle and drip it onto the edges to close the letter. Have an adult help you with this.

Make your own seal by cutting your initial into the end of a small round rubber. While the wax is hot, press your seal into it. Now the letter is safe. No one can open it without breaking your seal.

Alphabets and languages

How writing developed

1

Early people spread information by talking and telling stories. They also drew pictures.

2

The pictures developed into a written language. Each word had a picture to represent it. The Egyptians used this kind of writing. We call these word pictures 'hieroglyphs'.

3

The Babylonians developed the pictures into simple shapes that could be pressed into soft clay, using a wedge-shaped stick. We call this cuneiform writing.

4

Then someone invented an alphabet! It may have been a Caanite scribe who realized that there were only about 38 sounds in his language. If he made a simple sign for each one, he could make any word.

For instance, his word for fish began with a 'd' sound. So he drew a fish for the letter D. This was simplified later to a simple triangle shape.

Egyptian hieroglyphic writing, 16th C BC

	Canaanite	Phoenecian	Greek	Roman
fish				
man				
hand				
eye				

Many of the letters we use today, can be traced all the way back to the first alphabet.

The Rosetta Stone

Cracking the Egyptian code

No one in modern times could read early Egyptian picture language. Then, quite by accident, some soldiers discovered a very important stone. It had the same message written on it in two kinds of Egyptian and Greek. The experts were able to read the Greek. From that they could work out the meaning of the Egyptian writing too. The stone is called the Rosetta Stone. You can see it in the British Museum in London.

The languages of the Bible

The Bible was written in three main languages, Hebrew, Aramaic and Greek.

Most of the Old Testament is in Hebrew, the language of the Jewish people. ▶

◀ The books of Ezra and Daniel were written in Aramaic, the language of the Persian empire.

Project: Alphabets and languages

Make your own secret writing. Write the alphabet down one side of a piece of paper and then invent your own picture for each letter. You could use something that begins with that letter or a made-up squiggle. Use your secret writing to keep a private notebook. You may let your friends in on the secret and use your pictures to write notes to each other.

Have you read *How the Alphabet was Made* by Rudyard Kipling? It is a very funny short story about inventing an alphabet.

Being able to talk to other people is very important. The story of the Tower of Babel in Genesis 11: 1–9 shows this well. Try to imagine that suddenly you can't understand anything anyone says. What would it feel like? Write a poem about the story.

The New Testament was written in everyday Greek. ▶

Discovering the Bible

Real history

We can learn about the people who lived in a particular place long ago by reading what they wrote down and by studying the buildings and objects they left behind. The people who do this are called archaeologists.

One of their methods is to dig down into the mounds of earth and rubbish left behind where people have been living. They note carefully everything they find in each layer of earth. From this record, they can piece together a picture of what life was like in that place many thousands of years ago.

Because the Bible is a history of real people, archaeologists have been able to work on several of the places it mentions.

Project: Digging up the past

Have you tried digging for buried treasure in your own garden? You may only find pieces of old plate or plastic toys, but they all tell you something about our life today. Clean and display your 'finds' with a careful note of where they were found and the date.

You may be able to borrow or hire a metal detector and go hunting for buried treasure.

Try to find someone who has been to Israel. Ask them what they found out about the history of that country. They may have bought some modern-day pottery, or perhaps an old lamp made of clay that they could show you.

Look up Exodus 5:6–9. Does it give you a clue as to what the slaves in this scene from an Egyptian tomb are being forced to do?

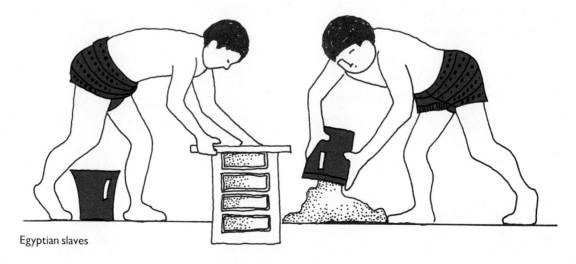

Egyptian slaves

This picture, carved on an obelisk, is thought to be Jehu King of Israel bringing tribute to King Shalmanasser III of Assyria. It is a remarkable find, as we have no other pictures of Old Testament characters.

Something to do

Some people have collected together everyday things from our own time and buried them in what are called 'time capsules'. They hope that people far into the future will find them.

Make your own time capsule. Find a good, watertight tin. Collect together everyday things that will tell people about you and your family. For example, you might include photographs, a list of your names and ages, a brochure showing where you went on holiday . . .

Wrap the items tightly in foil and put them in the tin. Seal the lid with masking tape. Now find a place to hide the tin in your house or bury it in the garden. Keep a note of where it is. You may want to find it again yourself in fifty years time!

The Dead Sea Scrolls

New discoveries about the Bible's history are still being made. In 1946 a shepherd found some large pots hidden in a cave near the Dead Sea. Inside the pots he could see many carefully-wrapped scrolls.

The scrolls turned out to be copies of every one of the Old Testament books except Esther. This was the library collected by a group of very religious Jews over 2000 years ago.

Who wrote the Bible?

The Bible is often called 'God's Word'. But God did not write it down himself or dictate it word-for-word.

Instead, he chose ordinary men and women who believed in him and learned about him through the things that happened to them. As we read their stories, or the poems or sermons they wrote, we can see God at work in real life.

But the Bible does say that God inspired them or caused them to write the truth. (The Bible's word for inspire is 'God-breathed', showing that he took an active part in what was written down.)

So the Bible is a unique book. It has special power to speak to people of every age and outlook. What it says can be trusted.

God chose some surprising people to pass on his message. Here are some of them.

Kings and princes

Moses was born an Israelite slave in Egypt. But he was adopted by an Egyptian princess and brought up in the royal household.

He was educated to be an Egyptian prince. But God had other plans. Moses was to lead the Israelites on the long, dangerous journey out of Egypt into freedom.

As well as being a great leader, Moses was able to use his education to write down his people's laws. You can find them in the first five books of the Bible.

When he became king of Israel, **Solomon** asked God to make him wise. God answered his prayer and Solomon became famous far and wide. Some of his poetry and wise sayings are collected in the Psalms, Proverbs and Song of Songs.

Daniel was a rich young man from a 'top' Jewish family. He was captured and taken away to Babylon, where he became an important advisor to the king. Daniel continued to worship God, even though it was dangerous in the foreign court. You can read his story in Daniel 6.

Shepherds and farmers

The man who wrote some of the greatest songs and poems in the world – the book we call the Psalms – began life as a shepherd boy. **David** was the youngest in a large farming family living outside Bethlehem. He later became King of Israel.

God called **Amos**, who was a farmer, to leave his sheep and his fig trees to become a prophet (or preacher). His sermons are recorded in the book of Amos.

Gospel writers

Four very different people wrote down the story of Jesus' life.

Matthew, tax man

Matthew was not a popular person. He made lots of money by collecting taxes from his own people and paying them over to the Romans.

One day, as he was sitting counting his money, Jesus stopped in front of him and said 'Follow me.' From that day on, Matthew travelled with Jesus.

Mark, a boy

Jesus and his friends used to meet in Mark's mother's house in Jerusalem when Mark was still a young boy. He would have listened to their talk and may even have been there when Jesus was killed. Later he became a follower of Jesus and travelled with both Peter and Paul. He may have had some help from Peter when he wrote down all that he remembered about Jesus.

Luke, doctor

Luke was a Greek-speaking doctor and a friend of Paul, one of the early Christian leaders. He may never have met Jesus, but he was a careful writer and found out all he could from other people. He also wrote the story of the first Christians, in the Acts of the Apostles.

John, fisherman

John and his brother James worked in their father's fishing business on Lake Galilee. Both left home to travel with Jesus, together with their friends Peter and Andrew. Later, James became leader of the Christians in Jerusalem. John wrote one of the gospels and several letters to the churches. He may also have written the last book in the Bible, called 'Revelation'.

Project: Reporting the truth

All four gospel writers were reporting what they knew about the same man and the same events. Yet each story is slightly different as it is told through the eyes of a different person. Read these four reports of Jesus riding into Jerusalem on a donkey and see how they differ. Matthew 21:1–11; Mark 11:1–11; Luke 19:28–40; John 12:12–19.

The same thing happens in the newspapers today. Collect several papers from one day. See how each one treats the same news story in a different way.

Be a reporter yourself. Ask your friends, separately, about a television programme they have all seen. See how many of them remember the main points. What about the details? If you have a portable tape recorder, interview them on tape and then play it back to the whole group.

Spreading the word

How our bible was put together

By the time of Jesus all the Old Testament books were well known and accepted. But their order was not finally agreed until the Jewish Synod (or meeting of religious leaders) at Jamnia in AD90.

2

Jesus used the Old Testament scriptures. He said 'Everything written about me in the Law of Moses, the writings of the prophets, and the Psalms had to come true.' Luke 24:44

Something to make

Try making your own collection of stories or poems, as a special present for someone. You will see how difficult it is to decide what to put in and what to leave out!

Copy what you have chosen into a small notebook and decorate the pages with drawings or patterns. Decorate the front and back covers with pictures you like.

Something to do

A newspaper editor is someone who decides what will go into the paper each week. Write and ask if you can visit your local newspaper and see how the editor does his/her job. You could be the editor of your own family newspaper. Write the news yourself, add some pictures and jokes and pass it around for everyone to read.

Into new languages

The Christians lost no time in spreading the good news about Jesus. Everywhere they went, they took with them the scriptures in Greek, and translated them into the languages of the people.

A man named Jerome made the earliest translation from Greek into Latin, the official language of the Roman empire. It took him twenty-one years!

3

Christian leaders wrote letters to encourage and help the first churches. They kept these letters.

The books about Jesus written by Matthew, Mark, Luke and John became the official accounts of his life and message.

Church leaders at two important Councils, held at Laodicea in AD363 and Carthage in AD397, finally agreed on which books should be included in the New Testament of the Christian Bible.

1

The Bishop of Edessa (in modern Turkey) translated The Bible into the everyday language of his people – Syriac. Missionaries from his church went as far as India and China using his book.

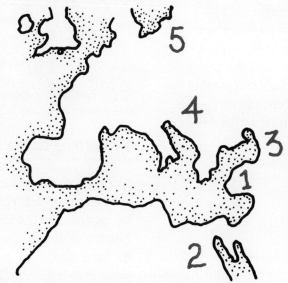

4

In the ninth century, two brothers called Cyril and Methodius went as missionaries to the people of Eastern Europe. The brothers invented an alphabet so that they could write down a Bible for them. It is the one still used today in Eastern Europe and Russia.

2

The first Christians in Egypt spoke Coptic, a language dating back to the ancient Egyptians. The Coptic Bible is still used by the church in Egypt. The language itself is no longer in everyday use.

3

Missionaries from Turkey went north into Armenia (now part of the USSR) and translated The Bible into Armenian.

Armenians then went to their neighbours in Georgia and made a translation for them.

5

The Ostragoths, living in northern Europe, had a Bible in their own language three hundred years after Jesus' birth. A famous copy of it is now kept in Sweden.

1000 Years in Latin!

The Latin Bible translated by Jerome became the standard Bible of the church for a thousand years. It was called the 'Vulgate' which means 'everyday language'. It was a Bible that everyone could read and understand. But as the Romans gradually lost their empire, Latin died out as the language of the people. Soon only the priests and scholars of the church could read the Bible. They used pictures and plays to teach people about God.

Beautiful books

The books that were made were very special. Every page had to be written out by hand and a whole book could take several years to copy. This work was usually done by monks, who made it their life's work. They decorated the pages, often using silver and gold and putting jewels on the covers. We call this work 'illuminating' manuscripts, which means to 'light up' with gold.

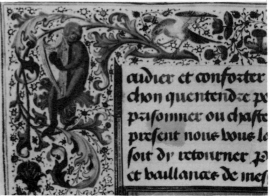

An illuminated manuscript

The Bible in English

During this time there were a few attempts to translate the Bible into Anglo-Saxon.

AD700 Aldhelm, Bishop of Dorset and Bede a monk in the north of England

AD871 King Alfred – parts of Exodus, Psalms and Acts

AD900 Wessex Gospels and Abbot Aelfric's first 7 books of the Old Testament

AD1200 Orm's Gospels and Acts in verse!

AD1384 John Wycliffe – The Bible in common English

Something to make

Many illuminated manuscripts from this time have surved. You can see some of the famous ones in the British Museum, London. Make an 'illuminated' name-plate for your bedroom door. Use a piece of good drawing card. Design a large capital letter and decorate it with patterns and borders. Add foil or sequins to look like 'jewels'.

Mystery plays

The church sometimes used drama to teach the people Bible stories. They began as dramatized Bible readings in church and soon grew into short plays. As they became more complicated, they were moved outside onto the church steps and finally into the market place. They were called 'mystery' plays because they taught religious truths. They were exciting entertainments. People watched and discussed them as we do programmes on television today!

Churches and pictures

The pictures and carvings in churches were more than just decorations. They were there to teach the people what the church believed. They were picture-sermons.

Something to make

Make a stained glass window card. Draw a simple picture on a piece of folded black paper. Cut out small shapes, leaving a black edge round each one. Stick coloured tissue paper behind each shape. Hang the card in a window so the light can shine through.

Something to make

Make your own mini theatre for a mystery play. Use a shoe box as a base. Staple a piece of light card around three sides and a strip along the top of the stage. Cut two doors at the sides of the stage and notches for scenery in the top.

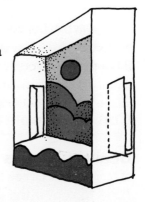

Draw a background for your favourite Bible story on a piece of paper. Tape it to a knitting needle and drop it in at the back of the stage. Decide on a simple Bible story, like The Lost Sheep, for your play. Draw and cut out the characters and push them on stage (using more knitting needles) to act the story.

Something to do

Some cities still perform their mystery plays from time to time. If there is one being acted near you, try and go to see it.

Into the language of the people

The church in Europe had enjoyed a long period of peace and quiet, when suddenly three events changed everything.

1. The Turks capture Constantinople (1453 AD)

The city of Constantinople was the home of many great Greek scholars. As the Turks took over the Greeks ran for their lives, taking their special books with them. This brought them into contact with those who wanted to write the Bible in everday words. The special books from Constantinople were a great help to them.

The city of Constantinople (now called Istanbul)

2. Rediscovery of the Bible's message

Because people had begun to study the Bible again, men like Martin Luther in Germany, Desiderius Erasmus in Holland, John Calvin in Switzerland and John Knox in Scotland used it to show what they thought was not right in the church. In time, this movement led to the split between Protestant and Catholic Christians.

This led also to a greater interest in the Bible itself. All over Europe, the work of Bible translation began.

3. Printing invented

In the city of Mainz, in Germany, Johann Gutenberg invented the printing press. Up to that time, each page of a book had to be carved out of a block of wood. The new press meant that pages could be made up quickly, from moveable letters. The first complete book printed in the western world was the Bible, in 1456.

Dangerous times

Gutenberg and his printing press

Not everyone was happy to see the Bible translated into everyday language. Leaders of the Churches felt threatened by this movement. The translators were often in danger for their lives.

In fourteenth century England, Oxford scholar *John Wycliffe* ordered the translation of the Latin Bible. Because of his work, he was forced out of Oxford in 1382 and lived in exile for the rest of his life.

Nearly a hundred years later, *William Tyndale* took up the task of preparing a good English translation. However, he was forced to go into hiding in Europe to finish the job. In 1536 he was betrayed and arrested in Belgium. His punishment was to be strangled and his body burned.

Project: Printing

There are all sorts of ways to print patterns and words on paper. The simplest is using a potato. Cut it in half. Mark a simple pattern on the inside surface. Carefully cut away bits of potato so that the design to be printed is raised. Dip the raised side in paint and press down on the paper. Make some colourful wrapping paper by repeating the pattern many times.

Try to visit a local printer to see how printing is done today. Raised metal letters are no longer used for most printing. Printers now 'set' type mainly by typing into a computer and photographing the typed words.

The Bible for the World

When James I became King of England the trouble over new translations of The Bible had begun to die down. The King ordered fifty translators to begin work on an official Bible which would be published with his full approval. It was called the 'Authorised Version'. It became the best-known English Bible for the next three hundred years.

After the explorers

The fifteenth century was the age of exploration. Men like Christopher Columbus and Vasco de Gama began to discover areas of the world unknown to the people of Europe.

Traders followed, bringing back exotic goods from North and South America, Africa, India, Japan and China. They also took along with them Christian chaplains and missionaries – and the Bible.

In the following 300 years, many missionary societies, both Protestant and Catholic, were set up. By the end of the nineteenth century Christian missionaries were working all over the world.

A European missionary in the 19th century

Mary Jones and the Bible Societies

By 1802 there was a great demand for Bibles in various languages of the world.

A group of Christian leaders met in London to discuss this need. A Welsh minister called Thomas Charles, stood up and told the group a true story:

'In my country, there is a girl called Mary Jones. When she was about eight years old, she heard some Bible stories read aloud. She loved them so much that she longed to have a Bible of her own.

So she learned to read. It took her six years, walking two miles to school every day. Then she saved up all her money and walked barefoot 25 miles to the town where I was selling the Bibles.

Sadly, on the day she arrived, tired and hungry, I had just promised the last Bible to someone else!'

Revd. Charles' story had a happy ending, however. He let Mary have the last Bible. The leaders decided to start a society to produce Bibles in as many languages as possible. They founded the British and Foreign Bible Society.

Other countries quickly followed and by 1907 there were over 8700 branches worldwide.

Wycliffe Bible Translators

In our own century, Bible translation has taken another leap forward with a society called the Wycliffe Bible Translators.

It began with a young American missionary called William Cameron Townsend. He was selling Spanish Bibles to the Indians in Guatemala, Central America. The Indians spoke a language called Cakchiquel (pronounced Catch-a-keel). One of them spoke to Townsend.

'If your God is so smart, why doesn't he speak my language?'

This challenge shocked the missionary. Immediately he set about translating the New Testament into Cakchiquel. It took him fifteen years.

We now know that there are more than 5000 languages spoken in the world. Fewer than 300 of these have a complete Bible translated, fewer than 1000 have a New Testament and fewer than 2000 have even one book of the Bible.

Today over 5000 people are working with Wycliffe Bible Translators all over the world.

Something to make

Make a languages bracelet for someone. Draw round a coin and cut several discs out of light card. Write the same word or phrase in as many different languages as you can. Write one word on each disc (for example LOVE, AMORE, L'AMOUR, LIBER, AGAPE etc.). Colour and decorate the discs and punch two holes in either side of each. Thread them onto coloured wool and tie the ends. Find someone who can speak another language. Ask them to teach you a few words.

Project: Different languages

Be a Bible translator. It's not as easy as you might think. Here is a list of words in Tampulma, the language of a tribe living in Northern Ghana.

a li	out
amaa	but
ba	their or them
be	son
dî	that
dí	eat
fune tum	sent
fun tum	did-send
hun-u	him
koosa	God
nara seria	people's judgement
ni	from
o	he or his
teene no maga	this-world's
tagna	bad
tum	works
wâ	not
wá	come
yisi	take out

See if you can make out what this verse from the Tampulma Bible is saying:

Koosa wâ fun tum o be dî o wá dí teene no

maga nara seria, amaa o fune tum hun-u dí

o wá yisi ba a li ba tum tagna ni.

(Answer on page 32)

27

Reading the Bible

There are no rules about reading the Bible. It is just like any other book. You read it any way you want.

But there is one important thing to remember. The Bible is more than just a book. It has been written so that people can learn more about God. God 'inspired' the writing of the Bible. So it *is* a special book. If you read it asking God to help you understand it, he will.

Remember, too, that the Bible is a library of books. Ask yourself these questions:

What kind of book is the one I'm reading?

What did it say to the people it was written for?

Why was it written?

What does it say to me?

Where to start

If you haven't read much of the Bible before, it's probably best to start with the story of Jesus.

Read the shortest Gospel – *Mark*. Or read *Luke's Gospel* and go on to *Acts* where Luke continues with the exciting story of the first Christians.

To get a taste of the Old Testament, try *Genesis*, which begins with some of the most famous Bible stories. *Exodus* continues the story of Moses (skip the bits about rules and laws). *Joshua* and *Judges* continue the story.

If you want a short story, try *Ruth, Esther* or *Jonah*. If you like science fiction, try *Ezekiel, Daniel* or *Revelation*. (You may not understand very much of these!)

Proverbs is full of wise and witty sayings. The *Psalms* are great prayers and songs, good for learning or reading aloud.

The letters in the New Testament are not easy to follow, but they do teach a lot about practical Christianity and what the early Christians were like.

Something to do

Get into reading the Bible for yourself. There are lots of different ways. Some people sit down and read a whole book of the Bible all at once. Others prefer to read a few verses each day and to think about what they mean before going on.

You might like to read and discuss it with other people in a school or church group, or with a friend. You could use it for bedtime reading with your brother, sister or whole family.

Something to make

Make a dramatic tape recording of a Bible story. Have some friends help you to read it and make background noises (like bells ringing, a donkey braying or people walking by). Play the recording back. The finished tape could make a good present for any young children you know.

Which version?

If you haven't already got a Bible, or you would like to buy a new one, it's hard to know which one to choose. Here is a short list of some of the best available at present:

New International Version
Slowly taking over from the *Revised Standard Version* as a good Bible for adults. There is also a children's edition – the same as the adult version but with pictures.

Good News Bible
Also called the *Today's English Version*. It is written in simple, everyday language so that people learning English can use it. There is a *Good News Children's Bible*, which leaves out the harder parts and is specially designed as a first Bible.

The Living Bible
Not a translation, but the Bible written by Kenneth Taylor in his own words. It is easy to understand. There is a children's edition and one for young people.

Revised Standard Version
A good, straightforward Bible for adults, but a bit hard to understand in places.

The Jerusalem Bible
The version approved by the Roman Catholic church. It also has some hard parts, but is great for reading aloud.

If you're the sort of person who can't get on with a lot of reading, you may prefer a book of Bible stories and pictures. There is also a Bible in comic strip, produced by David D. Cook Publishing Co. Some Bible stories have been recorded on tape and on record.

Something to make

Use a Bible story as a present. Make this pop-up Jonah and the Whale card.

Fold a piece of paper in half and then half again. Open it out again and make a cut across the fold at right angles. Make folds as shown.

Refold the card, pulling forward the folded pieces. Draw a large fish on the inside, using the cut as his mouth.

Now draw a small picture of Jonah inside the fish's mouth. Write the title on the front of your card. You could also write a short version of the story on the back.

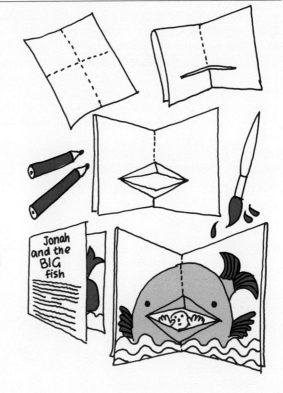

Bible puzzles

Old Testament wordsearch

All 39 Old Testament books are hidden in this wordsquare. They may be written forwards, backwards, up, down and diagonally (at a slant). Circle the words as you find them. We have marked 'Proverbs', to start you off.

```
B O J X L N O Z N T C M R F E J A U H S O J M
J S O M A B L U T V I W N B U X J K N M E L A
S D I F R O M X S C O B M D E L E O J R Y I L
K U K K A B A H A L M N G A L C O L M R U C A
E L I S E S T H E R E E L E W I S J A L D H C
O N E R Y P E T E N S H J E X O D U S E U R H
D 2 S A M U E L I W I E L L I A M S N I I O I
C K B A T T Z L H A I M E R E J E M I N K N H
E P O O L E E M A L C I O L M L E U M A S I A
P S A L M S K N J E N A I L B L A X L A D C I
N N D N F R I A Z E R H S E I A G G A H U L N
Y O Z A N N E N G M I C K U W I L L I A M E A
M I S J U D L E Y N M H S I S G N I K I C S H
O T I M O N N Z G U U O H T U R N N H C E L P
N A A I N E E R H N S S T I E P H A L A N G E
O T R E S E N A A N B E A C Y K I E A T E N Z
R N B I R I N A N R S A A U L R S I N G E R E
E E S G N I K 2 E S T E J S A I S A I A H V E
T M M I L Y N V P O L O L H A Y N F R A Z E R
U A N U T E O E M I N L C S Y D H A I D E B O
E L A N I R E L M A A E T R Y N B E N M A R Y
D A T W P I L L H T Z E S E L C I N O R H C 2
S G N O S F O G N O S O N Y N D I A N A H U D
```

New Testament teasers

The letters in the names of these New Testament books have been rearranged. Can you guess what they are?

SEW HERBS

CATS

I THY I TOM

RITE A NOVEL

LATIN SAGA

COINS A LOSS

Message from a star

Here is a secret message. See if you can decode it and discover who the mystery person is.

Message from a ☆

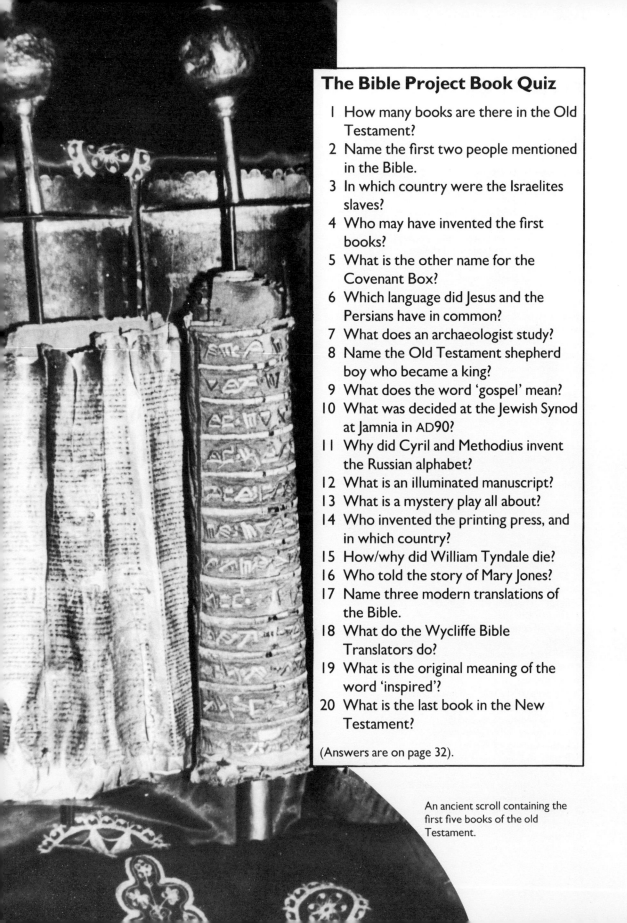

The Bible Project Book Quiz

1. How many books are there in the Old Testament?
2. Name the first two people mentioned in the Bible.
3. In which country were the Israelites slaves?
4. Who may have invented the first books?
5. What is the other name for the Covenant Box?
6. Which language did Jesus and the Persians have in common?
7. What does an archaeologist study?
8. Name the Old Testament shepherd boy who became a king?
9. What does the word 'gospel' mean?
10. What was decided at the Jewish Synod at Jamnia in AD90?
11. Why did Cyril and Methodius invent the Russian alphabet?
12. What is an illuminated manuscript?
13. What is a mystery play all about?
14. Who invented the printing press, and in which country?
15. How/why did William Tyndale die?
16. Who told the story of Mary Jones?
17. Name three modern translations of the Bible.
18. What do the Wycliffe Bible Translators do?
19. What is the original meaning of the word 'inspired'?
20. What is the last book in the New Testament?

(Answers are on page 32).

An ancient scroll containing the first five books of the old Testament.

Answers

Page 5

Pirate Jake's secret message reads: To find a treasure/go to/ the tower/at midnight.

The recipe is: 4oz butter
1 desertspoonful of honey
3oz sugar
2 eggs
4oz self-raising flour
½ teaspoonful baking powder
Spread with a little honey
and decorate with hundreds
and thousands.

Page 27

The verse is from John 3:17. The exact translation is: God not did-send his son that he come eat this-world's people's judgement, but he sent him that he come take-out them out their works bad from. The *New International Bible* puts it this way: For God did not send His Son into the world to condemn the world, but to save the world through him.

Page 30

New Testament teasers:
SEW HERBS = Hebrews
CATS = Acts
I THY I TOM = I Timothy
RITE A NOVEL = Revelation
LATIN SAGA = Galatians
COINS A LOSS = Colossians

Message from a star: '. . . the Bible is God's word to his creation, and for truth about him and about ourselves it is 100% reliable . . .' – Cliff Richard.

Page 31

The Bible Project Book Quiz
1 39
2 Adam and Eve
3 Egypt
4 The first Christians
5 The Ark of the Covenant
6 Aramaic
7 The things that ancient people left behind
8 David
9 Good news
10 The order of the Old Testament books
11 So that they could translate the Bible into Russian
12 A hand-decorated manuscript
13 Bible stories and religious truths
14 Johann Gutenberg, Germany
15 He was strangled and then burned for translating the Bible into English
16 Revd. Thomas Charles
17 Revised Standard Version, Jerusalem Bible, New English Bible, Good News Bible, New International Version.
18 Translate the Bible into more languages
19 God breathed
20 Revelation